CHANGING WORLD
AFGHANISTAN

AFGHANISTAN

Nicola Barber

Arcturus

This edition first published by Arcturus Publishing
Distributed by Black Rabbit Books
P.O. Box 3263
Mankato
Minnesota MN 56002

Copyright © 2008 Arcturus Publishing Limited

Printed in the United States

Library of Congress Cataloging-in-Publication Data

Barber, Nicola.
  Afghanistan / Nicola Barber.
      p. cm. -- (Changing world)
  ISBN 978-1-84837-004-3
  1. Afghanistan--Juvenile literature. I. Title.

  DS351.5.B36 2009
  958.1--dc22

                           2008016653

Series concept: Alex Woolf
Editor and picture researcher: Cath Senker
Designer: Ian Winton
Illustrator: Stefan Chabluk

Picture credits:
Corbis: cover left (Adrees Latif/Reuters), cover right (David Trilling), 8 (Natalie Behring-Chisholm/Reuters), 9 (Reza/Webistan), 12 (Alain DeJean/Sygma), 15 (epa), 23 (Reza/Webistan), 29 (Ahmad Masood/Reuters), 30 (Manca Juvan), 32 (Reuters), 38 (Arshad Arbab/epa), 42 (Syed Jan Sabawoon/epa).
EASI-Images (all Jenny Matthews): 14, 16, 17, 18, 19, 20, 21, 24, 26, 28, 31, 33, 34, 37, 40, 41, 43.
Topfoto: 11 (The British Library/HIP), 25 (Topham/Photri), 36.

The illustrations on pages 7, 27, and 41 are by Stefan Chabluk.

Cover captions:
Left: A Pashtun boy rides his mule past poppy fields at dusk near the southern city of Qandahar.
Right: Traffic in west Kabul.

Every attempt has been made to clear copyright. Should there be any inadvertent omission, please apply to the publisher for rectification.

Contents

CHAPTER 1

Introduction

In size, the country of Afghanistan is slightly smaller than Texas. It lies in the heart of Asia and is completely landlocked (enclosed by land). Its longest border is with Pakistan to the east and south. Afghanistan also has borders with Iran to the west and three Central Asian states to the north. It has a very short border with China in the mountainous northeast.

Landlocked and rugged

Roughly three-quarters of Afghanistan's landscape is mountainous and rugged. The ranges that dominate the center of the country include the Paropamisus and the Koh-i-Baba mountain ranges. Extending northeast from the Koh-i-Baba are the ranges of the Hindu Kush—the backbone of the country.

The airy peaks of the Hindu Kush include Afghanistan's highest mountain on the border with Pakistan (see box). Several high passes—routes that allow people and vehicles to travel through the mountains—cross this inhospitable land. The most important of these is the Salang Pass, which connects northern Afghanistan with Kabul to the south. A tunnel constructed in the 1960s cut down the time taken by vehicles to travel across this pass from 72 hours to 10 hours. At an altitude (height) of 11,152 ft (3,400 m), the tunnel is one of the highest in the world.

GEOGRAPHIC FEATURES

Area: 252,330 sq mi (647,500 sq km)
Border countries: China, Iran, Pakistan, Tajikistan, Turkmenistan, Uzbekistan
Coastline: none
Highest mountain: Noshaq, Hindu Kush 24,551 ft (7,485 m)
Major rivers: Amu Darya, Hari, Kabul, Helmand
Major cities: Kabul (capital), Qandahar, Mazar-e-Sharif, Herat
Source: *CIA World Factbook*, 2008

Plains and plateaus

North of the central mountain ranges lie the northern plains, which border Turkmenistan and Uzbekistan. The Amu Darya and numerous other, smaller rivers bring snowmelt from the Hindu Kush and the central mountain ranges to water fertile foothills and plains. Historically, this region has been a productive agricultural area, but recent conflicts have forced many farmers to flee their farms and pastures.

The southern lowlands have an average altitude of about 2,950 ft (900 m). This area, covering about 50,700 sq mi (130,000 sq km), forms part of the much larger Plateau of Iran, which also extends into Iran and Pakistan. Most of the land in this region is desert or semi-desert, although the Helmand River, which bisects the region, provides some water for irrigation (watering crops).

Climate

Afghanistan's location, far from the moderating influence of the sea, means that it has a continental climate—with some of the greatest extremes of temperatures in the world. In the mountainous regions, temperatures can drop as low as −13°F (−25°C) in the winter, while on the northern plains, summer temperatures in the daytime can rise as high as 115°F (46°C). In addition to seasonal extremes, temperatures often rise and fall rapidly between day and night. The Asian monsoon brings rain during the summer months to western Afghanistan, but the deserts of the southern lowlands remain hot and dry all year round.

This map shows the major towns and cities of Afghanistan and other places mentioned in this book. It also shows the mountain ranges that dominate a large part of this rugged country. The inset map indicates Afghanistan's location in the world.

People

In 2007, the population of Afghanistan was estimated to be 31,889,923. However, exact data for the number of people living in the country have long been unavailable because there has not been a nationwide census (official population count) since 1979. Even the 1979 census was unreliable because of conflict in parts of the country. Plans to hold a census were under way in 2008, backed by the United Nations (UN).

The people of Afghanistan come from a wide variety of ethnic backgrounds and speak many different languages. The majority of Afghans belong to one of two Indo-European ethnic groups, the Pashtuns and the Tajiks. The Pashtuns make up between 36 and 42 percent of the population and live mainly in the south and east. The Tajiks account for between 27 and 33 percent of the population and are found mainly in the northern provinces of Afghanistan. The next-largest ethnic group, the Hazaras, are about 9 percent of the population. They live in

Hazara women in the town of Bamian are caught by a strong gust of wind. The women run a bakery that provides rations of bread to elementary school children. The central region of Afghanistan, where many Hazaras live, is known as Hazarajat.

the central mountainous regions of the country. In the north are two Turkic groups, the Uzbeks and the Turkmen, who account for roughly 9

CASE STUDY: THE PASHTUNS

The Pashtuns make up the largest ethnic group in Afghanistan, and since the founding of the country in 1747 (see page 11), they have traditionally held the balance of power. Every ruler of Afghanistan from 1747 until 1978 was a Pashtun. However, the Pashtuns are themselves divided into tribal groups, with strong loyalties within the groups. Pashtun behavior is governed by an ancient set of laws called Pashtunwali ("the way of the Pashtuns"), which stresses family honor and vengeance for insults and also personal bravery and generous hospitality.

and 3 percent of the population respectively. Other minority groups in Afghanistan include the Aimak, the Baloch, the Nuristani, and the Pashai.

Languages

Both Pashto and Dari are the official languages of Afghanistan. Pashto is the language of the Pashtuns, and it is spoken by approximately 35 percent of the people. Dari is a form of the Persian language, often known as Afghan Persian or Afghan Farsi. It is used for business and government matters and is spoken by roughly 50 percent of the population. There are as many as 30 other languages spoken in the country, including two Turkic languages— Uzbek and Turkmen. Many people speak two or more languages.

Religion

The dominant religion in Afghanistan is Islam— 99 percent of the population is Muslim. The majority (about 80 percent) belong to the Sunni branch of Islam, while a minority of about 19 percent, mostly the Hazara community, are Shia Muslims. There are some groups of Hindus and Sikhs; the members of the small Jewish community have left the country. The Islamic religion plays an important part in the life of most Afghans, and mullahs (religious leaders) hold positions of some power in many communities.

A Pashtun boy sits on a hill south of Kabul. It is estimated that there are roughly 60 Pashtun tribes, organized into four larger groups.

CHAPTER 2

History

Afghanistan has been described by one historian as the "hub of the ancient world." Its geographical location at the crossroads of central, west, and south Asia has played a major part in shaping its history because settlers, travelers, and armies have all passed through. The earliest settlements in the region have been dated back to between 3000 and 2000 BCE, on the Plateau of Iran. Between 2000 and 1500 BCE, Aryan peoples migrated into the region. Some of them settled with their flocks of sheep and goats on the northern plains, while others established settlements in the region that is modern-day Kabul.

Ancient empires

During the reign of the Persian king Darius the Great (ruled 522–486 BCE), large parts of Afghanistan came under the control of the Persian Empire. However, Persian rule was constantly challenged by local peoples, and in 330 BCE, the Macedonian king Alexander the Great defeated the Persians. Alexander encountered somewhat more resistance as he tried to subdue the fierce peoples of Afghanistan.

After Alexander's death in 323 BCE, his vast empire was divided up, and much of Afghanistan came under the control of one of Alexander's generals, Seleucus. He established the Seleucid state in the north but lost territories in the south to the Indian Mauryan Empire. In 250 BCE, the Greek ruler of Bactria, a region in northern Afghanistan, declared independence from Seleucid rule. Greek influence in this area was to last until the arrival of the Parthians and the Kushans, and the Tajiks of northern Afghanistan trace part of their ancestry back to the Greco-Bactrians.

Muslims and Mongols

In 625 CE, armies from the Arabian Peninsula arrived in the region carrying with them news of a new religion—Islam. The Muslims conquered the Persian Sassanians who held power at that time, but the Afghan peoples were not so easily subdued or converted to the new faith. It was not until the tenth century that the first Islamic empire—the Ghaznavid dynasty, with its base at Ghazni near Kabul—was established in the region.

The arrival in 1219 of the Mongols, led by their ruler Genghis Khan, was catastrophic for the population of the region. The Mongols slaughtered thousands of people, destroyed cities, including Herat and Ghazni, and turned fertile land into desert by wrecking irrigation systems. The Mongol empire fell apart after Genghis Khan's death in 1227, was revived in the fourteenth century by Timur, and was finally defeated by the Mughals in 1526.

Afghanistan emerges

As part of the vast Mughal empire, Afghanistan was constantly being invaded and fought over by the Mughals, the Safavids to the west, and the Uzbeks to the north. In the eighteenth century, the Afghans (Pashtuns) rose against the Persian Safavids. In 1747, a Pashtun called Ahmad sought to unite the Afghan peoples against further invasion. Ahmad was elected shah (king), and throughout his reign (1747–72), he fought to create a kingdom that eventually covered much the same territory as modern-day Afghanistan.

This oval portrait shows Ahmad Shah Durrani (c. 1722–1772) wearing a green fur-trimmed coat and holding an ax. Ahmad Shah had 23 sons but on his death failed to say which one should succeed him. Over the following years, the princes plotted against each other while Ahmad's Afghan empire fell apart.

FOCUS: PEARL OF PEARLS

Ahmad Shah came from the Abdali tribe of the Pashtuns. When he was elected king, he adopted the title *Durrani*, "pearl of pearls." From that time on, the Abdali tribe were known as the Durrani.

The Great Game

In the nineteenth century, Afghanistan became caught between two world powers in what became known as the "Great Game." Britain was extending its influence across the Indian subcontinent, and Russia was seeking to establish control over central Asia. Tensions between the two countries led to two wars in Afghanistan (1839–42 and 1878–80) when the British invaded the country. In the 1890s, Britain and Russia between them drew up the boundaries of Afghanistan, which included a thin finger of land in the east, called the Wakhan Corridor, to act as a buffer zone (neutral area) between their two rival empires.

Independence

A third Anglo-Afghan war in 1919 finally brought Afghanistan independence from British interference in its affairs. King Amanullah

CASE STUDY: THE DURAND LINE

The Durand Line is the eastern border of Afghanistan that divides it from Pakistan. It is named after British diplomat Sir Mortimer Durand, who in 1893 negotiated the agreement for the border. However, the Durand Line runs directly through Pashtun territories and has never been accepted by any Afghan government. After the British created Pakistan in 1947, Afghanistan called unsuccessfully for the Pashtuns to have the right to set up an independent state, Pashtunistan, to reunite the territories divided by the Durand Line. The issue of the Durand Line continues to cause tension between Afghanistan and Pakistan to this day.

(ruled 1919–29) was the first king of the new nation. He and his successors, Nadir Khan (ruled 1929–33) and Zahir Shah (ruled 1933–73), concentrated on modernizing the country. Yet many of their reforms met with great resistance from Islamic religious leaders. Increased tensions with neighboring Pakistan over the Durand Line also attracted the attention of two world superpowers once again. This time Afghanistan turned to the Communist government of Soviet Russia (USSR) for support, while the United States backed Pakistan.

In 1973, a coup overthrew Zahir Shah. The new leader, Mohammed Daoud, abolished the monarchy (rule by a royal family) and declared a republic. He tried to reduce Afghanistan's dependence on the USSR, but pro-Communist groups within Afghanistan resisted. In 1978, Daoud was assassinated (murdered), and the new Communist government once more strengthened ties with the USSR. The government also tried to introduce radical reforms, for example, banning forced marriages and giving women the right to vote. These moves led to revolts across the country.

It was from this time that the anti-Communist armed fighters—mujahideen ("holy warriors")—emerged. In response to the political upheaval, the USSR decided to invade Afghanistan. In December 1979, it organized a huge airlift of thousands of Soviet soldiers into Kabul.

Delighted Afghan mujahideen stand on a Soviet helicopter they have destroyed in 1979. The mujahideen movement developed in response to the pro-Soviet government in Afghanistan in the late 1970s and the Soviet invasion of 1979.

Soviet occupation

The USSR occupied Afghanistan for 10 years, during which a fierce war was fought between Soviet and Afghan troops and the mujahideen. The mujahideen included people from many different groups in Afghanistan who were united by their opposition to Soviet rule. They were backed by the United States and other nations and used guerrilla tactics to terrorize Soviet and Afghan troops in the countryside. The intense fighting forced more than 3 million people to flee to neighboring Pakistan and Iran as refugees. Although the USSR controlled the cities, by the late 1980s, it had become clear that the war against the mujahideen could not be won.

These women were supplied with rifles by the USSR in order to fight against the mujahideen. The mujahideen were financed by many Western countries, notably the United States.

The mujahideen

In 1989, the USSR withdrew, leaving a weak Communist government led by President Mohammad Najibullah. However, the mujahideen, who had not been included in any of the negotiations that led to the Soviet withdrawal, continued to attack Kabul and President Najibullah's government. In 1992, President Najibullah resigned. The mujahideen entered Kabul and proclaimed the Islamic State of Afghanistan. Yet infighting between the mujahideen quickly led to chaos. Faced with daily violence, many Afghans began to support a new Islamic group, the Taliban.

The Taliban

The Taliban are a fundamentalist Islamic group (see page 16). In the early 1990s, many mujahideen joined the Taliban, attracted by their extreme commitment to Islam. Led by Mullah Mohammed Omar, in 1994, the Taliban captured Qandahar in the south, followed by Herat in 1995 and Kabul in 1996. They rapidly imposed their strict interpretation of Islamic law on the country. In 1997, many of the mujahideen who had not joined the Taliban formed the United National and Islamic Front for the Salvation of Afghanistan, more commonly known as the Northern Alliance, to oppose Taliban rule.

The end of Taliban rule came in 2001, when forces from the United States and its allies linked up with the Northern Alliance to defeat the Taliban. The involvement of Western troops was part of the US-led "War on Terror," sparked by the terrorist attacks on the World Trade Center in New York on September 11, 2001 (see page 24). By the end of

An old man carries his granddaughter as they pass by the remains of their destroyed village after the May 1998 earthquake.

November 2001, the Northern Alliance had taken Kabul, and the Taliban had fled either to Pakistan or to the mountains. In December 2001, an interim (temporary) government, led by Hamid Karzai and backed by the UN, was installed in Kabul.

FOCUS: THE 1998 EARTHQUAKES

In February and May 1998, two massive earthquakes shook northeast Afghanistan. Together, the earthquakes killed at least 6,000 people and left many thousands more homeless. They struck in a rugged region between the Hindu Kush and the Pamir mountains, which was under the control of the Northern Alliance. The mountainous terrain meant that helicopters or donkeys had to be used to reach many of the stricken communities, while freezing temperatures and lack of food made life extremely difficult for the survivors.

CHAPTER 3

Social Changes

The almost continuous conflict in Afghanistan since 1978 has caused the death of up to 1 million Afghans. It has also forced many millions of Afghans to flee their homes and to seek refuge in the neighboring countries of Pakistan and Iran. In the early 1980s, the vast majority of these refugees were Pashtuns who went to Pakistan to escape the Soviet occupation.

The origins of the Taliban

The Taliban movement originated in the madrassas (religious schools) in Pakistan, where Pashtun refugees studied the Koran. The word *talib* means "student"; *taliban* is the plural. Led by Mullah Mohammed Omar, the movement gained ground among Pashtun refugees. Its beliefs were based on an extremely strict interpretation of the teachings of the Koran, combined with the traditional codes of Pashtunwali (see page 8).

Many of its followers had spent much of their lives away from their home country and had therefore lost touch with the more tolerant forms of Islam that had traditionally been used to govern the people of Afghanistan.

Life under the Taliban

When the Taliban began to move through south and west Afghanistan in late 1994, many Afghans welcomed them. Afghanistan was being torn apart by fighting between rival mujahideen warlords, and the Taliban's promises of strong rule and peace seemed far preferable to many people. However, once the Taliban had taken Kabul, they began to impose their strict interpretations of Islamic law. They broadcast lists

Women in *burkas* line up for food aid at a distribution point in Kabul. Mesh across the eyes and nose allows a limited view for the wearer of the *burka*.

This photograph, taken in 1998, shows one of the Buddhas of Bamian before it was blown up by the Taliban in March 2001. The destruction of the Buddhas caused outrage around the world.

of regulations on Radio Kabul (renamed Radio Sharia) and created a religious police force to enforce them—the Department for the Promotion of Virtue and the Suppression of Vice. The consequences for those caught flouting Taliban regulations were severe: public executions, beatings, stonings, and amputations (cutting off hands and feet) became common occurrences.

The Taliban's rules had a disastrous effect on everyday life—particularly for the female population. When they went out, women were forced to wear the *burka*—a garment that covers the entire body from head to toe. They were forbidden to work outside the home and were separated from men on public transportation. Girls were prevented from attending schools or universities. Women were not permitted to seek help from male doctors, and because female doctors were not allowed to work, health care became almost impossible to find.

The Taliban's rules also extended to culture and the arts. The Taliban shut down television studios and movie theaters, and banned any form of music or dance. Using a strict interpretation of Islamic law that outlaws any depiction of a living being, they destroyed works of art in the Kabul Museum.

CASE STUDY: THE KABUL MUSEUM

King Amanullah founded Afghanistan's national museum in 1924. It once contained exhibits that spanned the country's long and colorful history. However, a combination of bombing and looting (stealing) had already severely depleted its collections when the Taliban took power. The museum's officials had painstakingly stored thousands of items in packing cases in a vault to try to save them. Yet in 2001, the Taliban used axes and sledgehammers to smash most of the remaining pre-Islamic statues and objects.

Even traditional pastimes such as flying kites and playing or listening to music were forbidden under the Taliban regime.

Children play in the ruins of buildings that have been damaged by the conflict in Kabul. After the end of Taliban rule in 2001, this was a common scene in many parts of the city.

Devastation

The end of Taliban rule came in 2001, but by that time, conditions in many parts of Afghanistan were desperate. There were thousands of internal refugees—people who had fled their homes to a different region of Afghanistan. Most of the country's infrastructure—roads, bridges, and irrigation systems—had been destroyed. Schools and hospitals had shut because of a lack of supplies and staff. In fact, the Taliban ban on women working outside the home had had an almost immediate effect on the country's schools and hospitals because the majority of teachers and a large number of doctors were women.

The UN and nongovernmental organizations (NGOs) had struggled to provide aid to the people of Afghanistan under the Taliban regime. Lacking even water to drink and somewhere to shelter, many people relied on aid from the UN or from NGOs. However, the Taliban viewed such aid with suspicion and in 1998 shut down the offices of the UN and most of the NGOs, despite the consequences for ordinary Afghans. At that time, life expectancy (the age people could expect to live to) was 45 years—one of the lowest figures in the world—and 159 babies out of every 1,000 born died before their first birthday—one of

TRANSPORTATION AND COMMUNICATIONS

Airports: 46 (12 with paved runways)

Roads: 21,565 mi (34,782 km) (5,102 mi, or 8,229 km, paved; 16,463 mi, or 26,553 km, unpaved)

Railroads: none

Telephones: 280,000

Cell phones: 2.5 million

Internet users: 535,000

Source: *CIA World Factbook*, 2008

to restrict wives and daughters from participating in public life. In 2007, at least half of school-age girls did not attend school.

Girls attend a school in a village on the Shomali plain, north of Kabul. Although girls once again have the right to attend school, many families in rural areas still prefer to keep their daughters at home to work in the house.

the highest figures in the world.

After the Taliban

The UN and NGOs returned to Afghanistan after the fall of the Taliban. Afghanistan desperately needed help from countries around the world, and a conference in 2002 pledged $4.5 billion to help to reconstruct the war-torn country. The money was given to aid in the resettlement of the thousands of refugees who had begun to make their way home, to allow the rebuilding of the country's infrastructure, to improve education and health care, and to start to clear the land mines that covered much of the countryside (see page 21).

In theory, life improved for women after the fall of the Taliban. Women and girls became free to work outside the home, to attend schools and universities, and to go outside without wearing the *burka*. However, the reality is often somewhat different. Particularly in rural areas, many families continue

City and countryside

Since 2002, much of the aid that was pledged to help Afghanistan recover has gone to the country's cities, particularly to Kabul. Yet despite some repairs, many of the residents of Kabul still live without electric power much of the time. Across the whole country, only 6 percent of the population has access to electricity. There is a similar problem with water. While 63 percent of people in the cities have access to water, in the countryside, this figure drops to 31 percent. War damage to wells and irrigation systems has not yet been repaired, and recent droughts (see page 28) have made the problem even worse. The number of refugees returning to their home villages has also increased the demand on already scarce water resources.

Health care

The years of warfare have devastated Afghanistan's health care system. It is estimated that only one out of every four people has access to even the most basic health facilities, and these services are concentrated in the towns and cities. In many rural areas, people are unable to reach any medical facility, and many suffer from treatable diseases such as malaria and tuberculosis. For women, the risks are even higher; one of the most dangerous things a woman can

New houses under construction in Kabul. Afghanistan lost one-third of all its homes during the years of conflict, and there is now a severe shortage of housing, particularly in the cities.

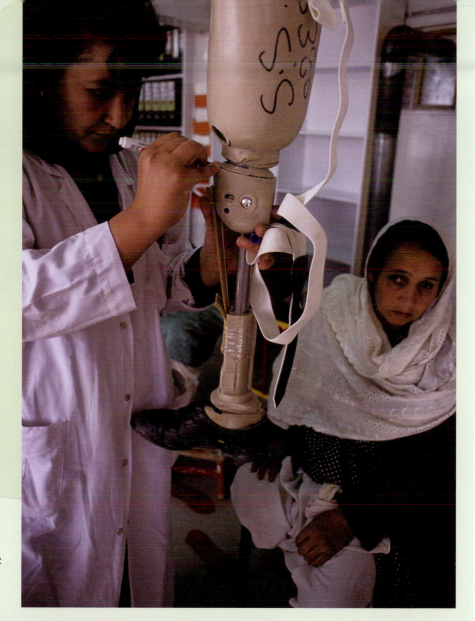

A doctor holds an artificial leg, which she will fit on a woman who lost her own leg in a land mine explosion. Land mines are a daily hazard for millions of people in Afghanistan.

do in Afghanistan is to give birth. Lack of basic facilities and equipment mean that 160 out of every 10,000 women die owing to problems during pregnancy or childbirth.

Mines and bomblets

Another legacy of conflict is the large number of injured and disabled people in Afghanistan. Some received their injuries during the fighting, but thousands of others have been killed or maimed by land mines. These small devices lie on the ground and explode when a person, an animal, or a vehicle

touches them. It is estimated that there are up to 10 million unexploded land mines in Afghanistan and that eight people every day are injured by these devices. In 2001, US aircraft also dropped cluster bombs as part of the campaign to remove the Taliban. These bombs send out small bomblets that, if they fail to explode on impact, pose a threat until they are disabled. Work to remove the mines and bomblets continues, but it is a long and dangerous process.

COMPARING COUNTRIES: HEALTH AND EDUCATION

Health and education have both suffered during Afghanistan's recent history. The literacy rate for women is the lowest in the world.

	Afghanistan	United Kingdom
Life expectancy	47	79
Infant (0–1) mortality (death) rate per 1,000	165	5
Child under five mortality rate per 1,000	257	6
Adult literacy rate, male	43%	99%
Adult literacy rate, female	13%	99%
Elementary school enrolement/attendance	53%	99%

Sources: UNICEF and *CIA World Factbook*, 2008

CHAPTER 4

Political Changes

Afghanistan is a country made up of many ethnic groups, and this fact continues to shape its history. Loyalties within tribal groups remain very strong, as do traditional tribal and ethnic practices. Despite the establishment of an elected government based in Kabul, Afghanistan remains politically fragmented since powerful and well-armed local warlords continue to assert their control over large parts of the country.

Ethnic violence

As the largest ethnic group in Afghanistan, the Pashtuns have traditionally held the balance of power in the country, although other ethnic groups have frequently challenged this position. The Taliban were mostly Pashtuns—although there were many Pashtuns in Afghanistan who did not support the movement or its politics. The Taliban mistreated and massacred other minority groups in Afghanistan, most notably the Hazaras, who follow the Shia form of Islam (Pashtuns are Sunni Muslims). Since the fall of the Taliban, it has been the Tajiks and Uzbeks who have dominated politics in Afghanistan. However, the country's head of state, Hamid Karzai, is a Pashtun.

The importance of religion

Alongside issues of ethnicity, the other factor that has influenced Afghanistan's politics throughout much of its history has been religion.

Islamic practices pervade all aspects of life in Afghanistan. The mullahs (religious leaders) not only conduct religious ceremonies and teach people about Islam, but also provide advice about a wide range of issues and help to solve disputes. In the past, many attempts to modernize the country or reduce the role of religion were strongly opposed by Islamic traditionalists. Islam provided the focus for opposition to the Soviet Communist government in the 1980s. Islamic practices were interpreted and enforced in an extreme way by the Taliban (see page 16), and it was during the Taliban era that Afghanistan became home to several fundamentalist Islamic groups, including Al Qaeda.

FOCUS: AHMAD SHAH MASSOUD (1953–2001)

Ahmad Shah Massoud was a Tajik who became a prominent military leader of the mujahideen. From his stronghold in the Tajik-dominated Panjshir Valley, in northern Afghanistan, Massoud masterminded the guerrilla war against the USSR during the 1980s. His mujahideen attacked fuel convoys on the Salang Pass and ambushed Soviet troops when they tried to advance into the Panjshir Valley. When the Taliban took power in 1994, Massoud became one of the leaders of the Northern Alliance. He was killed in a suicide attack on September 9, 2001, possibly by members of Al Qaeda.

Al Qaeda in Afghanistan

The leader of Al Qaeda, Osama bin Laden, was born in Saudi Arabia, but he came to Afghanistan in the 1980s to fight with the mujahideen against the Soviet occupation. During this time, he set up Al Qaeda, a terrorist group that aimed to oppose Islamic regimes its leaders believed were corrupt and to fight US influence in Islamic countries. Bin Laden returned to Saudi Arabia, but his increasingly extremist views and anti-government activities led to the loss of his Saudi citizenship. In 1996, Bin Laden returned to Afghanistan, where he forged a strong relationship with the Taliban leader, Mullah Mohammed Omar.

Ahmad Shah Massoud (center) rests, surrounded by his most trusted men. He was assassinated just a few months before the overthrow of the Taliban in December 2001.

Afghanistan became a center for Al Qaeda terrorist training camps, which drew volunteers from all over the world. In 1998, Al Qaeda members planted bombs near US embassies in eastern Africa. The United States responded by attacking suspected training camps in Afghanistan with cruise missiles (flying bombs). When the Taliban refused to hand over Osama bin Laden, the United States imposed economic sanctions (rules that made it hard for Afghanistan to trade with other countries), which were reinforced in 1999 by UN sanctions.

Terrorist attacks

On September 11, 2001, two hijacked aircraft crashed into the twin towers of the World Trade Center in New York. Another hijacked plane hit the Pentagon, in Washington, DC, while a fourth crashed into a field in Pennsylvania. The suicide attacks, which caused the deaths of nearly 3,000 people, were blamed on Al Qaeda. In response, the United States demanded that the Taliban shut down all terrorist training camps in Afghanistan and hand over Osama bin Laden. When the Taliban refused, the United States, together with troops from Britain, Canada, and several other NATO countries, linked up with the Northern Alliance to launch "Operation Enduring Freedom" to remove the Taliban from power.

Fighters at a former Taliban base in Jalalabad display leaflets offering a reward for information leading to the arrest of Osama bin Laden. The photo was taken in November 2001, shortly after the attacks on the United States.

Two fighter planes from the US Air Force fly over Afghanistan during Operation Enduring Freedom in 2001. The stated aim of this operation was to capture Osama bin Laden, destroy Al Qaeda, and remove the Taliban from power.

Political uncertainty

By the end of 2001, the Northern Alliance and the US-led coalition had taken the cities of Kabul and Qandahar from the Taliban. They did not, however, capture either Osama bin Laden or Mullah Mohammed Omar, and many Taliban fighters escaped to Pakistan, took refuge in the mountains, or simply disappeared back into the general population.

In order to try to stabilize the country, the UN invited Afghan leaders to a conference in Bonn, Germany, in November 2001. At this conference, an interim government was formed with representatives from the major groups within the country (including three women), to be led by Hamid Karzai. The interim government took power in Kabul in December, but the political situation remained extremely unstable. After years of fighting, the country was full of weapons, and many rival warlords had their own private armies. In addition, international troops continued to hunt down members of the Taliban and Al Qaeda.

The next stage of government, an emergency Loya Jirga (Grand Council) that took place in June 2002, was an attempt to broaden the government to try to include the various warlords and tribal leaders who held power in the regions. Under tight security, the Loya Jirga met in Kabul to form a transitional (temporary) government for Afghanistan. Its members elected Hamid Karzai as the interim head of state until elections in 2004.

FOCUS: THE LOYA JIRGA

A Loya Jirga is a tradition that extends back many centuries in Afghanistan. It is a meeting attended by representatives of the different peoples and ethnic groups in order to settle disputes, discuss problems, or approve new ideas or reforms. In 1747, a Loya Jirga elected Ahmad Shah Durrani as a new leader (see pages 11–12). In 2002, about 2,000 delegates from all over the country attended the Loya Jirga in Kabul. The Loya Jirga of 2003–2004 drafted and approved a new constitution for Afghanistan.

People in Mazar-e-Sharif gather to elect delegates to the Loya Jirga. Forty-one percent of the people who registered to vote in the presidential elections of October 2004 were women.

Establishing strong government

In January 2004, another Loya Jirga approved a new constitution, which became the official law of Afghanistan. The constitution established a strong presidential system in which the people directly elect the president and two vice presidents for five-year terms. At presidential elections held in October 2004, Hamid Karzai received 55.4 percent of the vote; he was sworn in as president in December.

In September 2005, the first parliamentary and provincial elections for more than 30 years took place. As set out in the constitution, the new National Assembly has two houses. The Wolesi Jirga (Lower House) has 249 seats, which are directly elected by the Afghan population. Of these, 68 are reserved for women. The Meshrano Jirga (Upper House) has 102 seats, 68 of which are elected by provincial and local councils and 34 of which are appointed by the president.

In 2005, some members of parliament (MPs) were angry that former warlords had been permitted to stand as candidates. One woman MP, Malalai Joya, expressed her opinion after the first session of parliament: "I see the future of this parliament as very dark because of the presence of warlords, drug lords, and those whose hands are stained

AFGHANISTAN KEY POLITICAL FACTS

Country: Republic of Afghanistan
Date of constitution: January 4, 2004
Political divisions: 34 provinces
Right to vote: Men and women age 18 and up

with the blood of the people." However, former Afghan king Zahir Shah remarked, "I thank God that today I am participating in a ceremony that is a step toward rebuilding Afghanistan after decades of fighting."

Disarming armed groups

Afghanistan's new government has faced many challenges, including continuing opposition from the Taliban and Al Qaeda, the booming trade in illegal drugs (see page 30), and the corruption and violence of the country's powerful warlords. Many of these warlords were funded and armed by the United States during the fight against the Taliban and subsequently refused to disband their private armies. There have been frequent clashes between rival warlords over territory, and many have used threats or violence to control local populations.

After the fall of the Taliban, it was estimated that there were about 1,800 illegal armed groups in Afghanistan, accounting for up to 100,000 individuals. Backed by the UN, in 2005 the Afghan government introduced the Disband Illegally Armed Groups (DIAG) program to allow soldiers to leave these groups and reintegrate into society. In 2006, it was reported that about 63,000 soldiers had been disarmed, of whom 55,000 were retrained. Some of them chose to enter Afghanistan's professional national army or police force, while others were being helped to set up small businesses, become farmers, or learn to clear land mines.

This diagram shows the three branches of government in Afghanistan: the executive, the legislative, and the judicial. The president and vice presidents are elected for five-year terms, with a maximum of two terms.

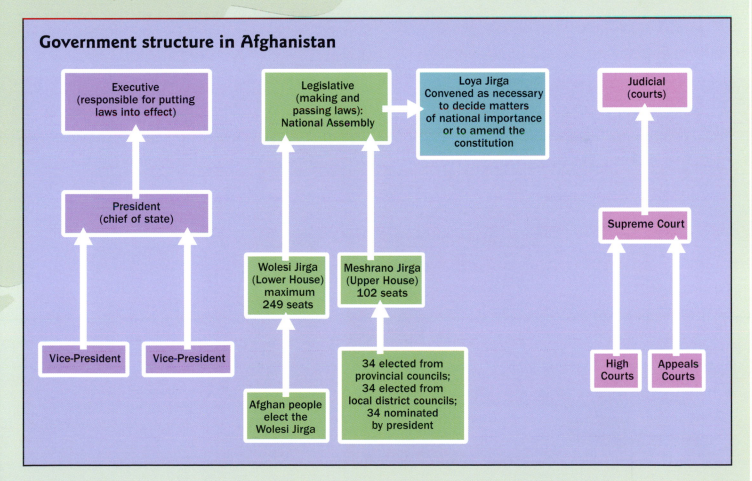

Government structure in Afghanistan

Executive (responsible for putting laws into effect)

President (chief of state)

Vice-President

Vice-President

Legislative (making and passing laws): National Assembly

Loya Jirga Convened as necessary to decide matters of national importance or to amend the constitution

Wolesi Jirga (Lower House) maximum 249 seats

Meshrano Jirga (Upper House) 102 seats

Afghan people elect the Wolesi Jirga

34 elected from provincial councils; 34 elected from local district councils; 34 nominated by president

Judicial (courts)

Supreme Court

High Courts

Appeals Courts

CHAPTER 5

Economic Changes

Afghanistan is one of the least economically developed countries in the world. The years of war have taken their toll, disrupting trade and transportation links and making it impossible for people to lead a normal life. Earthquakes and droughts have added to the country's problems. However, the economy has improved significantly since the fall of the Taliban. With the backing of international aid, the Afghanistan government has launched programs to create jobs, rebuild the country's infrastructure, and modernize its agriculture and industry.

An agricultural economy

In 1978, before the Soviet invasion, Afghanistan grew enough crops to feed its population and to supply a flourishing export market. Today, Afghanistan remains a largely rural country: about 80 percent of the population make their living from agriculture. The years of warfare, however, have disrupted agricultural production, and many Afghans continue to rely on food aid from international NGOs in order to survive. Afghan farmers are faced with several problems, including the need to rebuild irrigation systems, the huge numbers of land mines that make areas of fertile land unusable, and, in recent years, drought. In desperation, many farmers have turned to a traditional crop grown in Afghanistan—poppies (see page 30).

During the drought of 2006, children collect water from a pipe and prepare to load the heavy plastic containers onto their donkey. Drought has been a major problem in recent years.

A man stands by his sheep at a livestock sale in Kabul in 2006. Livestock, including cattle, sheep, goats, donkeys, camels, and horses, is a vital source of income for many Afghan families.

Only 12 percent of Afghanistan's land is suitable for growing crops, and less than half of this amount is regularly cultivated. Wheat has traditionally been the most important food crop, but wheat harvests have been severely affected by the droughts that crippled the country in the early 2000s. Even in 2003, when Afghanistan produced its best wheat harvest for 25 years, the country still needed to import wheat to fulfil its needs, and many people relied on food aid in order to survive. Other important food crops include barley, corn, rice, and cotton. Afghanistan is famous for its sweet grapes, and raisins are an important export. Farmers grow other fruits such as melons, apricots, cherries and figs and also nuts.

About 46 percent of the country's land area is meadow or pastureland (with grass for animals), and livestock is vital to rural communities. In northern Afghanistan, karakul sheep are bred for their tight, curly fleeces. The trade in karakul pelts from newborn lambs is reviving after almost shutting down during the Taliban era.

COMPARING COUNTRIES: GNI AND GDP

Compare Afghanistan with its near neighbor Pakistan, and it becomes clear that years of conflict have affected Afghanistan's economy. Gross national income (GNI) is the total value of goods and services produced within a country plus income received from other countries. Gross domestic product (GDP) is the total value of goods and services produced within a country.

	Afghanistan	Pakistan
Gross national income (GNI) per capita	$250	$690
Gross domestic product (GDP) per capita annual rate of growth	1.6%	3%
GDP by sector	Agriculture, 38%; Industry, 24%; Services, 38%	Agriculture, 19.6%; Industry, 26.8%; Services 53.7%

Source: UNICEF

The opium economy

Opium poppies have long been grown in Afghanistan. The poppies produce opium, which is used to make the illegal drug heroin. Afghanistan has become the major supplier of heroin worldwide. In 1979, Afghanistan produced roughly 220 tons (200 metric tons) of opium; by 1999 this amount had increased to 5,060 tons (4,600 metric tons). Then in 2000, the Taliban banned poppy cultivation completely. As production suddenly dropped, the worldwide price of heroin rocketed. The Taliban put surplus Afghan stocks on the market and

A family at work in a poppy field in Badakhshan. All the family work, including children when they are not in school. The ripe poppy heads are cut to allow the valuable opium gum to ooze out. The gum is then collected and sold to produce heroin.

AFGHANISTAN KEY OPIUM ECONOMY STATISTICS

A 2007 survey of nearly 3,000 Afghan farmers in 1,500 villages across Afghanistan revealed the following facts:

28% of these farmers had never grown opium poppies because it was against their Islamic beliefs.

16% did not grow opium because it is an illegal crop.

16% did not grow it as a result of instructions from the elders in their communities.

16% did not grow it because of a fear that the government would destroy it.

Of those who did grow opium:

29% grew the crop to reduce poverty.

25% grew it because of its high sale price.

Source: United Nations Office on Drugs and Crime, 2007

Farmers near Kabul winnow wheat to separate the grain from the stalks. Wheat is an important crop in Afghanistan and provides an alternative to growing poppies. However, wheat crops have been hard hit by the recent droughts.

sold them at a high price.

After the fall of the Taliban, the ban on poppy cultivation in Afghanistan remained. Yet many farmers, driven to desperation by drought and poverty, began to plant the crop again. Poppies flourish in a dry climate and provide a much-needed source of income. By 2004, poppy cultivation was recorded in all the provinces of Afghanistan for the first time. In some places, so much land was being used to grow poppies instead of food crops that the food supply was threatened. Increasingly, heroin is being produced inside Afghanistan itself for export to Western countries. In 2004–2005, opium earned $2.8 billion for Afghanistan—more than the total amount of aid to the country in that period.

In addition to being illegal, a large proportion of the wealth from the opium economy goes to just a small number of people—warlords and drug traffickers (dealers in illegal drugs). They use some of this money to maintain their independence from the central government, posing a threat to the fragile political stability of the country. In 2004, the Afghan government established the Ministry of Counternarcotics and started to introduce various schemes to reduce the cultivation of poppies. The top priority is to provide farmers with an alternative means of earning a livelihood. The government is also targeting opium stores, heroin laboratories, and drug traffickers to strengthen law enforcement.

A survey published in 2007 by the UN and the Ministry of Counternarcotics outlined a new development in the opium economy. That year, Afghanistan produced 9,020 tons (8,200 metric tons) of opium and became almost the only supplier of heroin worldwide. In fact, the country's production now exceeded world demand for the drug. However, in central and

FOCUS: PRECIOUS STONES

People have been mining precious and semi-precious stones for thousands of years in Afghanistan. Gemstones were transported along the ancient trade routes that ran across Afghanistan to far-flung civilizations in Mesopotamia, Egypt and India. Today, emeralds are found in the Panjshir Valley, rubies and sapphires in the Jegdalek region in Kabul Province, and lapis lazuli high in the mountains of Badakhshan Province in the north-east.

north Afghanistan, despite massive poverty, the cultivation of poppies had decreased, and 13 provinces in this region were opium free.

In southwest Afghanistan, the story is somewhat different. By 2008, Taliban rebels had retaken control of large areas of land. About 70 percent of the country's poppy crop comes from five provinces in this region, and 50 percent is grown in just one province—Helmand. It was difficult to see how the opium economy could be overcome unless the Afghanistan government regained control of these regions.

Natural resources and industry

Although the mainstay of the Afghanistan economy is agriculture, the country has considerable natural resources, including natural gas, oil and coal, and mineral deposits such as copper, talc, zinc, and

The Afghan president, Hamid Karzai (left), with the Turkmen president (center) and the Pakistani prime minister (right) at the ceremony in 2002 to sign an agreement to build a gas pipeline across the three countries.

semiprecious stones. Natural gas was exported to the Soviet Union during the 1980s, but production was hit by the years of war and instability. In 2002, Afghanistan signed an agreement with Turkmenistan and Pakistan to allow a pipeline to be built across Afghanistan to carry gas from Turkmenistan to Pakistan. The pipeline could earn hundreds of millions of dollars per year in the form of transit fees (amounts paid to Afghanistan for allowing the pipeline to run across its territory). However, the continuing violence in Afghanistan means that there are still major obstacles to be overcome before work could start on the pipeline.

Gemstones are another important natural resource. Emeralds, rubies, and lapis lazuli are all found in Afghanistan. Most of these stones are exported illegally to Pakistan, where they are sorted. The best-quality gems are then sent elsewhere to be precision-cut for Western markets, which means that Afghanistan obtains little profit from this precious resource. In 2005, the Afghan government passed new laws to regulate the mining industry, with the aim of modernizing it and legalizing the trade in gems.

Industry is on a small scale and includes the production of textiles, leather products, soap, furniture, fertilizer, and cement. Carpet making is the most important handicraft industry. Afghan carpets are made of wool, silk, or cotton and are woven or knotted by hand, mostly by women. It is estimated that there are more than 1 million workers in this industry. Most of the carpets are taken to Pakistan to be "finished" (cut and washed) before being exported to Europe and the United States.

CHAPTER 6

Environmental Changes

Life in Afghanistan's dry and mountainous terrain has never been easy. Yet 25 years of armed conflict has had a devastating effect on Afghanistan's environment and on the people who rely on the land to make a living. Military activities, including the use of chemicals and land mines, have left large areas of land unsafe and unusable. The movement of internal refugees from one part of the country to another has damaged the land, resulting in some areas being abandoned and others being overused.

A deminer uses a knife to explore ground that is known to be mined. He will remove any mines he finds. This painstaking and dangerous work is the only way to make mined areas safe again.

CASE STUDY: THE SISTAN WETLANDS

The Helmand River ends in a large region of marsh called the Sistan wetlands. This region is shared by Afghanistan and Iran, and at times of good water supply, it covers about 1,560 sq mi (4,000 sq km). This area has been an important area for agriculture for thousands of years, with large irrigation schemes to water crops and cattle grazing in the reed marshes. It is also an area teeming with wildlife, particularly migrating wildfowl. However, in the drought that hit Afghanistan in 1998-2003, the water in the Helmand River was reduced to 98 percent below its annual average and the Sistan wetlands almost completely dried out.

The almost complete breakdown of government meant that there were no controls over, for example, where people extracted water or where they grazed their herds. In addition, the recent years of drought have severely affected the country's water supplies.

One region that illustrates the appalling legacy of years of war is the Shomali plain, about 19 miles (30 km) north of Kabul. This area of about 585 sq mi (1,500 sq km) was once a thriving agricultural region, often described as the "orchard of Kabul." But it has been a battleground for more than two decades and is now desolate and windswept.

Water and drought

Water is a precious resource in Afghanistan. The country's rivers have their sources in its mountains and drain into five main drainage basins. The Amu Darya rises in the Pamir mountains and forms much of the northern boundary of Afghanistan. The longest river in Afghanistan, the Helmand, rises in the Hindu Kush and runs across the southwest plains before ending in the wetlands of the Sistan Basin.

Afghanistan's water supplies rely almost entirely on the snowmelt that feeds these rivers and on the country's rather unreliable rainfall.

From 1998 to 2003, levels of rainfall were exceptionally low, resulting in severe drought. Another drought in 2006 brought further suffering to the Afghan population. In drought-affected areas, people were unable to irrigate their crops, leading to severe food shortages. Millions of people suffered from lack of food, and many died—especially children.

In some places, lack of water has forced people to try to tap sources farther underground by sinking deeper wells. Without a coordinated plan to control such water extraction and without adequate rainfall to renew supplies, these wells only deplete the groundwater even more. Drought has an impact on the land surface too. With no plants to hold it in place, dried-out soil is easily picked up and carried by the wind. Windblown sand and dust can fill in canals and irrigation ditches and cover roads and houses. In the Sistan wetlands (see box), sandstorms completely covered up to 100 villages during the drought of 1998–2003.

Deforestation

Afghanistan's forests are another precious resource that is under increasing pressure. Forests of oak and conifers are found in the eastern part of the country, along the border with Pakistan in the regions that tend to have higher rainfall. In the central and northern regions, pistachio and almond trees provide important sources of income for many people, while in the southwest regions, scrubland (low shrubs and grasses) grows in the drier areas. Forests are home to a wide variety of animals, including snow leopards, flying squirrels, and black bears.

A reforestation project to replace pistachio trees in the province of Samangan, northern Afghanistan. The forests were cut down by desperate villagers during the years of war.

In the 1970s, local governments controlled the cutting down of pistachio trees and the harvesting of pistachio nuts. However, during the years of conflict, these controls broke down. Local people were forced to cut down many trees for fuel. In some places, military forces also removed large numbers of trees for fuel or because they provided possible hiding places for ambush. In the forests along the Pakistan border, illegal logging (cutting down trees) remains a problem. The cedar trees in these forests provide valuable wood for uses such as furniture making. Despite a ban on logging, this activity continues, and many people in the region rely on it to make a living. Cedar timber fetches a high price in Pakistan, so much of the wood is illegally exported and sold there.

Deforestation is a major issue because cutting down trees is not only the loss of a valuable resource, but has other serious effects. On hillsides, trees help to protect the ground from rain, and their roots hold the soil in place. When the trees are cut down, this protection is removed, and heavy rain often causes floods and landslides. In both 2006 and 2007, floods and landslides claimed many lives in Afghanistan.

COMPARING COUNTRIES: DEFORESTATION

Both Afghanistan and its neighbor Pakistan face similar problems with deforestation. Forests in Pakistan are being felled for the same reasons as in Afghanistan—the need for fuel and illegal logging.

	Afghanistan	Pakistan
Total forested area	2,141,490 acres (1.3% of total land area)	4,697,940 acres (2.4% of total land area)
Deforestation 1990–2005	1,091,740 acres (33.8% of forested area)	1,543,750 acres (24.7% of forested area)
Total number of animal species	694	1,027
Threatened species	31	56

Source: Mongabay.com

Urban pollution

Although Afghanistan remains a country with a largely rural population, problems such as desertification and deforestation are driving many people into the cities. Returning refugees are also adding to urban populations. After years of warfare, and with violence a continuing threat in many areas, environmental conditions in Afghanistan's cities are poor. There are problems with access to clean water, sanitation and waste disposal, and air and water pollution.

Sewage systems are very basic in most of Afghanistan's cities. Dirty water often flows down open sewers (ditches) in the streets before running into the nearest canal or river. Because this dirty water is not treated to make it safe, cross-contamination—when dirty water infects the clean water supply—is common. Waste disposal poses another threat to health. Waste piles up in the streets or is taken to dump sites. Dangerous waste, such as medical waste from hospitals, is often mixed with household waste, and many dump sites are in unsuitable locations. The UN and NGOs are working with the Afghanistan government to try to address these issues for the future.

A woman and children who have no running water in their homes collect water from a pipe in Kabul. Sanitation and access to clean water are major problems in Afghanistan's cities.

37

CHAPTER 7

Changing Relationships

When the Taliban held power in Afghanistan, only three countries in the world officially recognized the regime: the United Arab Emirates, Pakistan, and Saudi Arabia. Other countries objected to the Taliban's brutal crushing of human rights and became increasingly concerned about the rise of extreme Islamist groups such as Al Qaeda within Afghanistan.

After the fall of the Taliban in 2001, Afghanistan once more became an active member of the international community.

Afghan refugees load their possessions onto the back of a truck as they leave their refugee camp in Peshawar, Pakistan, in 2006, ready to return to Afghanistan. Many Afghans have lived in Pakistan for decades.

FOCUS: RETURNING REFUGEES

Pakistan became home for millions of Afghan refugees from the late 1970s on. Many refugees who were born in Pakistan had never seen their homeland until the Afghans began to return home in 2002. The UN has helped the refugees. Returning families have received some money, their children have been vaccinated, and they have been educated about the dangers of land mines. In 2002 and 2003, it is estimated that 1.9 million Afghan refugees were assisted by the UN to return home from Pakistan.

Nevertheless, for many people, the return to a homeland they have not seen for up to 20 years has been a huge shock. A lack of basic services and few opportunities for paid work have meant an uncertain future for many former refugees.

Afghanistan and Pakistan

Afghanistan has long had an uneasy relationship with its neighbor Pakistan. One of the main sources of tension between the two countries has been the issue of the Durand Line (see page 13), which has caused problems between the two countries since Pakistan was created in 1947. The presence of extreme Islamist groups in the border regions is a more recent problem.

The Durand Line has played a major part in Afghanistan's history. The governor of Paktia, one of the provinces adjoining the Pakistan border, observed: "The reason that Afghanistan adopted friendship with the Soviets was for Pashtunistan . . . and the result was, we did not gain Pashtunistan, but we almost lost Afghanistan."

The Afghan government under President Karzai has not issued a formal policy on the Durand Line, although like other Afghan governments in the past, it refuses to recognize it as an international border. Meanwhile, in 2005 President Pervez Musharraf of Pakistan proposed building a fence along the border in order to mark exactly where it runs—although the precise position of the border is itself a matter of dispute in many places. He also proposed laying land mines along the border, but such a move is strongly opposed by the Afghan government.

Pakistan found itself in a difficult position after the fall of the Taliban regime: the Taliban movement had originated in Pakistan, and Pakistan had supported its regime. Yet after the terrorist attacks on the United States of September 11, 2001 (see page 24), Pakistan became committed to helping the United States in its "War on Terror." Pakistan sent thousands of troops into the border regions to hunt down members of the Taliban and Al Qaeda. Nevertheless, Afghanistan continues to accuse Pakistan of sheltering Islamist extremists, who cross over into Afghanistan to commit terrorist attacks.

Most ordinary people living on either side of the Durand Line simply want to be able to make a living and to travel freely from place to place. There are some hopeful signs: in 2006, a daily bus service began between Jalalabad in Afghanistan and Peshawar in Pakistan. This "friendship" bus is the first cross-border service for nearly 30 years. More generally, at meetings between Presidents Karzai and Musharraf in 2006 and 2007, both sides stressed the need for the two countries to work together to improve relations, to fight against terrorism, and to strengthen trade between their countries for the good of both their economies.

Iran and Afghanistan

Unlike Pakistan, Iran actively opposed the Taliban regime and supported the Northern Alliance. Since 2001, relations between Iran and Afghanistan have improved, although there is an ongoing dispute about the levels of water reaching Iran in the Helmand River. Another area of tension concerns the numbers of Afghan refugees still in Iran. During the 1980s and 1990s, roughly 2.4 million Afghans fled to Iran. Since 2002, Iran has encouraged these refugees to return home, and more than 1.6 million have done so. However, many remain unwilling to risk going

A patrol of US troops leads a group back from prayers during the Muslim Id festival in the town of Khost, near the Pakistan border. The United States has the largest number of foreign troops in Afghanistan— about 15,000 in early 2008.

back to an insecure future in their homeland. Reports in 2007 that Iran was forcibly deporting refugees led to protests from the Afghan government and the UN. It was subsequently agreed at a meeting between UN officials and the governments of the two countries that refugees could return voluntarily until March 2008.

OVERSEAS AID

Countries around the world have given aid to help with the reconstruction of Afghanistan. The total aid received in 2005 was $2.775 billion.

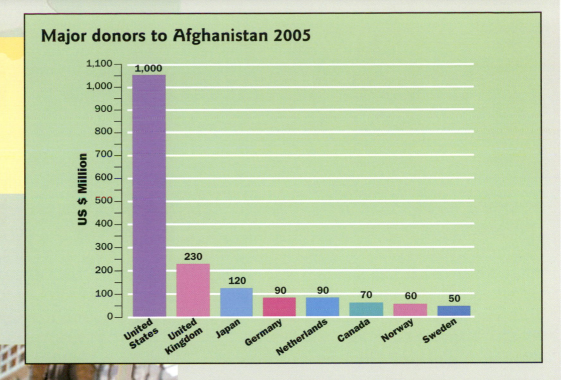

Major donors to Afghanistan 2005

US $ Million

- United States: 1,000
- United Kingdom: 230
- Japan: 120
- Germany: 90
- Netherlands: 90
- Canada: 70
- Norway: 60
- Sweden: 50

The international coalition

After the fall of the Taliban, the UN established an international force in Afghanistan. Led by NATO, in 2007 the International Security Assistance Force (ISAF) was made up of about 41,700 troops from 39 different countries. Initially, ISAF's aim was to gain control of Kabul and its surrounding area from the Taliban. Since 2003, however, the UN has given permission for ISAF to expand its mission across the country to provide security and to help with reconstruction. ISAF is also helping to train the new Afghan National Army and police force as well as helping the Afghanistan government with its DIAG program (see page 27). Nevertheless, continued fighting with the Taliban has meant that large areas of Afghanistan are still in effect war zones.

A woman in Kabul is registered for her monthly food aid distribution from the charity CARE, an organization that helps to fight global poverty. While the economic situation remains so grave, such aid is vital for many people in Afghanistan.

CHAPTER 8

Future Challenges

In November 2007, several MPs visited the northern town of Baghlan to attend a ceremony to reopen a sugar factory. The MPs were meeting people, including groups of children, outside the factory when suddenly a huge bomb exploded, killing at least 41 people, including six MPs. Although it is not known for certain if the attack was a suicide bombing or if the Taliban carried it out, it was one of hundreds of similar attacks in Afghanistan that year.

Since 2001, the Taliban has continued to fight a guerrilla war against the government in Afghanistan. The Taliban can still rely on a large amount of support in rural areas, where its type of justice appeals to many in the more traditional

Afghan policemen gather around the wreckage of a vehicle at the site of a bomb blast on the outskirts of Kabul in late 2007. A remote-controlled bomb planted on the road blew up the vehicle, killing its four Afghan passengers.

Women practice their computer skills. New opportunities have opened up for many women in Afghanistan, but continuing conflict, poverty, and opposition to women's rights from people with traditional views are all great challenges for the future.

communities. Many Afghans have also become disillusioned with President Karzai's government, with the slow pace of reconstruction in the country, and with the presence of foreign troops. The Taliban has in effect taken control of large areas of the countryside and since 2006 has increasingly used suicide bombers to disrupt daily life in the towns and cities and to scare local populations.

Relationships between local people and the foreign troops have also reached the breaking point on occasion. In May 2006, a US military truck lost control and rammed into rush-hour traffic in Kabul. Five people were killed and others were injured in the crash. The accident sparked an anti-US riot among onlookers, during which at least 14 more people died. Many Afghan people feel that some foreign troops are too careless with the lives of Afghan civilians.

Key issues for the future

In January 2008, a report by the US-based Afghanistan Study Group warned that progress in Afghanistan was under threat from "resurgent [growing] violence, weakening international resolve, mounting regional challenges, and a

growing lack of confidence on the part of the Afghan people." It stated that the international community was trying to win the war in Afghanistan with "too few military forces and insufficient economic aid." It also warned that the Afghan government still had little control over the regions beyond Kabul and that the Taliban, the opium economy, and the "stark poverty" faced by most Afghans were the main challenges to be faced in the future.

HOPE FOR THE FUTURE?

A 2008 report by an NGO called the International Crisis Group outlined several key areas for action:

- Stronger international leadership by the UN
- Better international coordination, and better coordination between civil and military groups in Afghanistan
- Ensure a full, adequately funded commitment of troops for as long as needed
- Aim to stabilize the Afghan state and its institutions by cracking down on corruption
- Rethink policies toward Pakistan to end its role as a haven for the Taliban

Source: International Crisis Group, 2008

Timeline

3000 and 2000 BCE Earliest settlements in Afghanistan.

2000 and 1500 BCE Migration of Aryan peoples to the region.

522–486 BCE Afghanistan comes under the control of the Persian empire.

c. 330 BCE Alexander the Great takes control in Afghanistan.

323 BCE Alexander dies. Period of Seleucid and Greco-Bactrian rule.

c. 625 Muslim armies bring Islam to the region.

962–1140 Ghaznavid dynasty.

1219 Mongols invade Afghanistan.

1526 Babur establishes the Mughal empire.

1747 Ahmad Shah Durrani is elected king.

1839–42 First Anglo-Afghan war.

1878–80 Second Anglo-Afghan war.

1919 After the Third Anglo-Afghan war, Britain recognizes Afghan independence under King Amanullah.

1933 Zahir Shah takes the throne.

1956 Close ties between Afghanistan and USSR established.

1973 Coup overthrows Zahir Shah; Mohammed Daoud declares a republic.

1978 Daoud is assassinated; pro-Soviet Communist government is set up.

1979 Soviet troops invade Afghanistan; start of civil war between Soviet and Afghan troops and mujahideen.

1986 Mohammad Najibullah becomes president.

1989 Soviet troops withdraw.

1992 Mujahideen overthrow government of President Najibullah.

1996 Taliban captures Kabul and control most of the country.

1998 Massive earthquakes in the northeast; US air strikes against Al Qaeda in Afghanistan.

2000 UN imposes sanctions on Afghanistan

2001 Interim government under President Karzai established.

2002 Loya Jirga elects Hamid Karzai as president.

2003 NATO takes over security operations in Afghanistan.

2004 Loya Jirga approves a new constitution; Hamid Karzai wins presidential elections.

2005 Parliamentary elections held; DIAG program set up.

2008 More NATO troops sent to Afghanistan to try to keep the country from sliding into civil war.

Glossary

Aryan Describes the Asian peoples who in prehistoric times settled in what are now Afghanistan, Iran, northern India, and Pakistan.

burka A garment worn by many Muslim women in Afghanistan that covers the entire body from head to toe.

Communist The system of government in the Soviet Union (1922–91), where the government controlled the production of goods and the running of services.

constitution A set of laws governing a country or organization.

continental climate The typical climate in the center of a large area of land; very hot summers and very cold winters are typical features.

coup The overthrow of a government, often by force.

deforestation Cutting down so many trees that forests cannot grow back.

desertification The process by which an area changes into desert because of lack of rainfall and increased demands on the land from the local population.

drought A long period with little or no rain.

ethnic group A group of people who share a culture, tradition, way of life, and sometimes language.

fundamentalist Describes a movement that stresses a strict interpretation of a set of rules, for example, in religion or politics.

guerrilla To do with a group of fighters that make war against a regular army.

Indo-European Describes speakers of Indo-European languages, which include the major languages of Europe and much of Asia.

land mine A small explosive device, placed on or just under the ground, that is set off when a person, an animal, or a vehicle touches it.

Loya Jirga (Grand Council) In Afghanistan, a meeting attended by representatives of the different tribes and ethnic groups in order to settle disputes, discuss problems, or approve reforms.

monsoon A seasonal wind. In Asia, the monsoon brings annual rainfall to India and southeast Asia during the months of June to September.

mujahideen ("holy warriors") In Afghanistan, the fighters who emerged in response to the Communist government and the Soviet invasion in the late 1970s.

NATO Stands for North Atlantic Treaty Organization, a military alliance of 26 countries from North America and Europe.

nongovernmental organization (NGO) An organization that is independent of government control.

occupation Moving into another country and taking control of it using military force.

Pashtunwali ("the way of the Pashtuns") An ancient set of laws that govern Pashtun society, which stress family honor, generous hospitality, and personal bravery.

republic A state without a king or queen.

sanitation The provision of facilities to dispose of human waste safely.

Shia Describes Muslims who follow the Shia branch of Islam. Shia Muslims believe that religious authority can lie only with direct descendants of the prophet Mohammad.

suicide attack An attack intended to kill others in which the attacker knows that he or she will also die.

Sunni Describes Muslims who follow the Sunni branch of Islam. Sunni Muslims believe that religious authority lies with the person best able to uphold the customs and traditions of Islam.

Turkic Describes people who originate from speakers of the Turkic languages. The Turkic language family is made up of roughly 30 languages, including Turkish, which are spoken across eastern Europe, Central Asia, and western China.

warlords Independent military leaders in different regions who each try to extend their power.

Further information

Books

Adams, Simon. *Countries in the News: Afghanistan.* Smart Apple Media, 2007.

Banting, Erinn. *Lands, Peoples and Cultures: Afghanistan, the Land.* Crabtree Publishing, 2003.

Behnke, Alison. *Visual Geography Series: Afghanistan in Pictures.* Lerner, 2003.

Downing, David. *Witness to History: Afghanistan.* Heinemann Library, 2004.

Englar, Mary. *Countries and Cultures: Afghanistan.* Capstone Press, 2006.

Kazem, Halima. *Countries of the World: Afghanistan.* Gareth Stevens, 2002.

van der Gaag, Nikki. *World in Focus: Afghanistan.* World Almanac Library, 2007.

Woodward, John. *Opposing Viewpoints: Afghanistan.* Greenhaven Press, 2006.

Websites

http://news.bbc.co.uk/1/hi/world/south_asia/country_profiles/1162668.stm
BBC website with country information and links to the latest news in Afghanistan.

www.afghanistans.com/
Links to information about Afghanistan's history, geography, people, and news.

www.afghan-web.com/
General site with information about many areas of Afghan life.

www.unicef.org/infobycountry/afghanistan.html
Information on Afghanistan on the UNICEF website, with a focus on children.

Index

Page numbers in **bold** refer to illustrations and charts.